UNLOCK YOUR CAGE

Elaine La Monica Rigolosi

ISBN: 1463772750
ISBN 13: 9781463772758
Library of Congress Control Number: 2011913481
CreateSpace, North Charleston, SC

I dedicate this book to my father, Richard Anthony,
who painted memories in my childhood
that frame my life
and will live with me
forever.

I dedicate this book to my mother, Carrie,
who I always remember as having endless drive,
who believed anything was possible, and
who taught me to feel my own power.

I dedicate this book to my treasured husband
and forever friend, Bob,
who always encourages me and helps me
to follow my dreams and
to give them life.

$\mathscr{T}$ABLE OF CONTENTS

$\mathcal{I}$NTRODUCTION

This story is designed to help you become aware of changes that you may wish to make in your life. These changes may be one-time events or may span your lifetime—conquering a bad habit, losing weight, achieving goals in education, attaining a new position or a promotion, developing a new exercise program, training for athletic events, and so forth.

The intent of this book is to illustrate that life is a series of choices, given your unique blend of reality. There are aspects in your life that were given to you by birth and during your early years. What you do with your gifts and circumstances, however, is and should be accomplished by conscious choices, using your own power from within. You are in control of how you view the island on which you stand at any and all given points in time. Your unique island can be expanded or viewed in a positive perspective or in a negative perspective—by your own control. In essence, you put on the eyeglasses that frame what you see. You can choose the eyeglasses, for example, that give you the vision of whatever you want to see. You can lead yourself to where you wish to be.

If you have realistic goals and you have the desire to achieve them, you have everything needed to make changes in your life successfully and to view life positively. Life involves choices, and you can choose to view your circumstances in a positive way and summon your own power to achieve your goals, or you can feel helpless, caged, and out of control.

Using directed self-control of one's thoughts and behavior as examples, I have written this book as an allegorical fable that shares a process for becoming aware of your thoughts, driving forces, and inner strengths and then focusing them toward goals by using the power of imagery. The characters are allegorical creatures who live on a lake. Their homes contain symbols of what is in your home, according to your individual and personal interpretations. The story is an interwoven tale of professional and personal feelings and of experiences that reveals in the final fabric the various textures involved in being human.

Both children and adults can enjoy and understand the allegory; the meanings derived from the allegory, however, are intended to deepen with maturity.

Perhaps an ideal beginning scenario is for an adult to read the book to a child...then read it again...and again...as desired....

Elaine La Monica Rigolosi

The Lily Pad Was Shrinking

"I just do not understand what's happening," Gretchen moaned, looking sadly at Hans. "We've measured the leaves, and they're the same size as before...nothing has changed. Ever since we made our new picnic baskets and created our Well of Many Spirits on The Leaf Branch we started noticing trouble. Now Little Gretel and Little Chaunce love picking extra foods and small goodies and keeping them in their baskets. It is all very convenient, too, because when we're hungry, we don't have to search for food or snacks—we have storage now—but, *that* should not make our Lily Pad shrink!"

Hans shook his head, looking confused and dismayed. This was becoming a serious problem, and feeling as though he was the head of his home, he felt responsible and frustrated. While thinking, he dipped into the picnic basket for some of the berries preserved and coated in sugarcane. Mmm, he thought as he tried them, no wonder Little Gretel loves these. They sure taste good, especially when I'm upset and need to think. They also calm me and make me feel better for a little while.

Gretchen busied herself preparing dinner. It was Great Harvest Day on The Lake and celebrations were in order. Lily Pads were decorated with ferns, violets, and maple-sugar drops, the traditional ornaments of the season. Playful children hopped from one Lily Pad to another in anticipation of the food and treat festival that was the hallmark of the holiday. Everyone lovingly made specialties and shared them with friends.

Gretchen and Hans had invited the Freddies over for the Great Harvest Day celebration. Preparations had taken days and—for some things—months. Hans and Little Gretel had hunted and planted while Gretchen and Little Chaunce had cooked and created, tasting and trying out everything as they worked to be sure that all was as delicious as anticipated. Of course, they had often shared samples with Hans, Little Gretel, and their friends.

A rippling of water in the distance announced the arrival of guests. Gretchen, Hans, Little Chaunce, and Little Gretel leaped to the edge of The Lily Pad and watched as the Freddies arrived. Hugs, kisses, and expressions of good cheer marked the beginning of the holiday festivities.

Finally, after an array of miniature welcoming treats, the two families sat down at The Great Harvest Leaf.

Gretchen had arranged the foods on The Leaf delicately and beautifully, as an artist might mix colors to show love, riches, happiness, and security. The Leaf contained more holiday specialties than could ever be consumed in one night, but the items were all symbolic, and those present respected, admired, and enjoyed them. Everyone tasted a little of everything, eating and drinking heartily, smiling, leaping with glee, and offering each delicacy full attention. Little Chaunce and Little Gretel, however, were not allowed anything from The Well of Many Spirits because they were too young.

The Great Harvest Day dinner lasted late into the night—much longer than usual gatherings. The last ripple melted into The Lake after the Freddies swam for home. Gretchen and Hans decided they were so full that a rest was in order on The Leaf Branch next to The Well of Many Spirits. Little Chaunce and Little Gretel had fallen asleep already.

The array of goodies on The Great Harvest Leaf did not hold its sparkle anymore, but it would be terrific to sample the leftovers after a nap and during the following days. All foods could be stored in the picnic baskets now, and nothing would be wasted. Little Chaunce especially loved to snack during his bedtime story, and whenever anyone got up at night, a tiny tidbit always seemed to be the ideal sleeping pill. Everyone felt warmly toward the picnic baskets, and the food inside them was always ready for snacking. The Well of Many Spirits was especially welcoming to grown-up guests.

Gretchen and Hans smiled as they talked. The holiday had met all their expectations. Their friendship with the Freddies seemed better than ever. Little Chaunce and Little Gretel were not teasing each other beyond reason. Gretchen felt wonderful about her growing abilities as a homemaker, cultivator, and cook, and she was especially content with her new career as a pattern-maker for picnic baskets. Also, Hans was becoming a better hunter, fisherman, and gardener every day. Nothing went to waste. This made Hans feel most successful and gratified. Little Gretel and Little Chaunce were learning what interested them. Little Chaunce had taken up artistic painting, and Little Gretel was a natural in gymnastics.

There was only one problem in the home—The Lily Pad was shrinking! The size of their home became a major concern when Gretchen tripped over Little Chaunce one day on The Leaf Branch, the stem of The Lily Pad, throwing Little Chaunce off balance. After taking one step backward, Little Chaunce fell off The Leaf Branch and into The Lake. His fall frightened Little Chaunce so much that Gretchen had to jump into the water to rescue him, even though he was instinctively a good swimmer. Gretchen struggled to lift him up onto The Lily Pad, and then she climbed home herself. After they were both safe and secure, Gretchen noticed how tired and out of breath she felt.

Gretchen reflected on the good old days when she had been a champion swimmer and Hans had been the best long-jumper. They had met at the yearly Lake Challenge competition. Gretchen understood that age does indeed slow one down a bit, but she was frightened by the thought that she might become unable to protect her family when they needed her. She had worried that she would become a poor role model for Little Chaunce and Little Gretel. In a sense, she had felt helpless. So she had decided to talk with Hans about it that evening.

In preparation for the discussion, Gretchen made Hans's favorite foods, and, as planned, they talked well into the night over The Dinner Leaf. Then they put Little Gretel and Little Chaunce to sleep and sat on The Leaf Branch by The Well of Many Spirits. They both sipped their drinks slowly. Both Gretchen and Hans seemed comforted, and their fears were quieted by the goodies they munched on as the hours passed.

After tossing around many ideas and thoughts, Gretchen and Hans finally decided that they might have a problem that required some outside guidance. So they decided to visit The Great Wizard of The Lakes for help.

Then they slept.

After a good breakfast the next morning, Gretchen, Hans, Little Chaunce, and Little Gretel set out for The Lily Pad of The Great Wizard of The Lakes. Even though it took longer than expected to swim there (since everyone had to rest often), the journey was pleasant.

The Great Wizard of The Lakes had a family of four who, from a distance, lived on what seemed to be a large Lily Pad with many Leaf Branches that glided playfully over the water. In keeping with tradition, Hans threw a flower onto The Great Wizard's Lily Pad as a request to visit. The Great Wizard eagerly picked up the flower and waved. Hans, Gretchen, and their little ones then climbed up.

Strangely, once everyone was on The Great Wizard's Lily Pad, Gretchen thought it did not seem so large and spacious. Thinking about the shrinking Lily Pad she shared with Hans, she quickly concluded that things might simply look smaller as one grows older or as things become more familiar. That notion was perplexing. But since there was little time to think, and she and Hans were already there to ask for help and get answers, she dismissed the thought.

After an exchange of greetings, The Great Wizard of The Lakes escorted his guests into a special area where they could have privacy. After everyone had chosen a spot and had gotten comfortable, he offered them Water Petals filled with sparkling water and smiled warmly. "I know that you have come for a special reason," The Great Wizard of The Lakes said, "and I would like to listen to you."

Hans related the problem of their shrinking Lily Pad. As Hans talked, Gretchen sipped water from her Water Petal, and she quietly enjoyed the refreshment after the long swim. She also felt very welcome, noting the full attention given by The Great Wizard, as expressed by his gaze and physical movements.

After Hans finished talking, The Great Wizard of The Lakes sat back thoughtfully. The Great Wizard did not speak immediately.

The Great Wizard's silence made Hans nervous, so he picked up his Water Petal and drank. The water and the movement calmed his tensions by giving him something to do. He glanced around for something to nibble and something different to drink. He found nothing and then thought wistfully of his Well of Many Spirits, wishing that it was close.

At last, The Great Wizard of The Lakes spoke. "I believe I can help you, and I am willing to put forth my time and share my knowledge regarding 'Unlocking Your CAGE.' I will provide this information to you in four Lessons, the first starting tomorrow and the other three each day thereafter. Please go home to your Lily Pad and consider my offer. If you return tomorrow, I will assume that you are committed to and will attend all Lessons, and I will begin to share the Lessons with you."

Hans and Gretchen thanked The Great Wizard of The Lakes profusely, eagerly promising to return. All smiled as they parted.

Later that evening at home, Hans asked Gretchen, "Do you know anything about the knowledge regarding unlocking cages?"

"No," Gretchen replied. "It sounded strange to me. I have no idea what The Great Wizard of The Lakes meant."

Hans shook his head skeptically while reaching for some fresh pieces of sugar cane gumdrops and something else from The Well of Many Spirits. Sensing his hesitancy about The Great Wizard's proposal, Gretchen suggested that they visit The Great Wizard the next day to find out what he meant by "cage," at least for one Lesson. "Certainly," she said, "we have no reason not to—except, of course, the swim will be long and tiring."

Hans nodded in agreement while raising an eyebrow. He felt that Gretchen's suggestion of going for one Lesson would satisfy his curiosity, though it sparked guilt for the lack of commitment to all four Lessons that The Great Wizard expected.

After a few deep moments of thought, Hans looked at Gretchen and nodded in submission. "Okay," Hans replied. "Let's try!"

The next morning, Hans and Gretchen left Little Chaunce and Little Gretel with neighbors and set off to visit The Great Wizard of The Lakes. The little ones, they figured, would be able to learn from them whatever they thought was important. Leaving plenty of time for the journey, they decided to bring their picnic basket and to stop along the way for a hearty breakfast. The Warmth in The Sky gave them a bright yellow day. Gretchen and Hans swam slowly as they glanced around at the scenery, and they arrived exactly on time.

COMMITMENT

THE FIRST LESSON

COMMITMENT

The Great Wizard of The Lakes exchanged friendly morning greetings with Gretchen and Hans. Once they were comfortable and sipping from their Water Petals, The Great Wizard's eyes and movements signaled the beginning of The First Lesson.

In a voice and a manner of great authority and wisdom, The Great Wizard stood and handed Gretchen and Hans each a book full of blank Memory Leaves. He asked that these serve as workbooks for The Lessons— both for instructions and for notes. Offering special and colorful Writing Stems, The Great Wizard asked that Gretchen and Hans start at the first page and write down five important accomplishments in each of their lives that made them proud.

After Hans and Gretchen had finished writing, The Great Wizard of The Lakes listened to them explain their lists and then commented on their achievements.

Gretchen and Hans each happily shared memorable experiences. Gretchen noted how she had gotten up before the sun every morning for six months so that she could practice swimming without interruption while training for the National Swimming Championship at The Lake Challenge competition. Hans shared how he had practiced jumping over Water Bushes between continuous speed swimming. He believed that this extra effort had resulted in his becoming The Long-Jump Champion of The Water Universe, since he had broken all previous records and no one had ever matched or bettered his record.

The Great Wizard of The Lakes then led Gretchen and Hans into discovering the ingredients that made up their successes. Through their conversation with The Great Wizard, Gretchen and Hans realized that their goals had been met because they were *committed* to the goals and gave *energy* to their accomplishments.

After the review of their achievements, The Great Wizard of The Lakes sat back thoughtfully. "You see," he then explained, "in each of us there are three aspects: *what we think*, *what we feel,* and *what we do*." He paused and changed his seating position. "In order to accomplish anything in an optimal fashion, these three aspects of ourselves must work in harmony toward an identified goal that is realistic."

The Water Petals were refilled, and then The Great Wizard continued. "*What we think* happens in our heads.

Others truly never know *what we think* unless we are consciously aware of our thoughts *and* we choose to share them with others. Some of the things we think about include our goals, needs, and desires. *What we feel* are our emotions, and they are expressed both inside and through our bodies. Our emotions have a lot of energy. Sometimes our emotions are visible only within ourselves. Sometimes we show them to others and are aware of what we are doing. And sometimes our feelings show by their own direction. When others perceive our emotions and our thoughts, together or separately, this is our behavior. Behavior has its own language—through our body movements and through the words we use. Behavior is *what we do*. It involves action. Thoughts and feelings cannot speak or share; they remain silent unless we share them with others."

Even though he seemed to still have much to say, The Great Wizard paused, silently sipping from his Water Petal, and then pondered a moment as if framing another image. Finally, he said, "Harmony within us occurs when our thoughts, feelings, and behaviors move toward the same goal." Looking at Gretchen and Hans in turn, he added, "Most likely, you both accomplished those great things you just spoke of because, first, you strongly desired to do them—this happened in your thoughts. Second, you really got excited with the ideas of what it would feel like to achieve your goals—these were your feelings. Next, and

third, you directed your behavior toward your goals—
what you did to accomplish your dreams. The more these
three aspects work in harmony, the higher the probability
that we will succeed—quickly and effectively."

Hans and Gretchen nodded with understanding, but
tiny, unspoken questions such as "What does all of this
have to do with our shrinking Lily Pad?" remained. By
his response, The Great Wizard of The Lakes seemed to
perceive their questions.

"Let me explain how the information I have shared
connects to why you are here and to the importance of The
First Lesson," The Great Wizard said. "In our present and
immediate environment, we have The Lake, The Lily Pad,
and each one of us as individuals. Everything that occurs
is related to each of these aspects working—reacting to
and acting toward one another. For example, it would
be difficult for us to lie still on The Lily Pad if there was
great movement in The Lake. The Lily Pad would ripple in
response to the water's movement, and we would be jostled
no matter how quietly we sat. We could sit so that The Lily
Pad was balanced and thereby have an effect on quieting
The Lake, but we could never lie as still as we could if The
Lake were calm and we all agreed to sit balanced on The
Lily Pad. Commitment to ourselves and then to each other
is also very important."

A sparkle came into The Great Wizard's eyes. "It is also
possible to exaggerate the movement of The Lake—like

this." And he unexpectedly jumped from one place to another, flipping his Water Petal so that it splashed on Gretchen and made her grin and jump backward. "You see, everything plays a part in the eventual outcome. Our movements, individually and as a group, have an effect on The Lake and on each other. The Lake equally has an effect on us."

A glimmer of awareness appeared on Hans's face. "You mean," he asked, "our shrinking Lily Pad may be a response to something happening in The Lake?" Hans paused, took a deep breath, and then added with deeper feeling, "It may also have something to do with *us* at the same time?"

Looking at his guests, The Great Wizard nodded. "Yes. That is exactly my point! It will be necessary to explore your unique situation—both of you individually, as well as Little Chaunce, Little Gretel, your Lily Pad, your part of The Lake, and your friends—in order to become aware of why you believe your Lily Pad is shrinking. This process takes commitment. You must want to understand. The idea of becoming aware and in control must excite you, and you must promise to follow through with, think about, and complete all four Lessons."

After his last statement, Gretchen felt that The Great Wizard knew what she had said to Hans about trying only The First Lesson. She shared nothing at that point, looked down, and doodled something on a Memory Leaf.

Now The Great Wizard of The Lakes became emphatic. "Most important, you must both promise yourselves, each other, and me that you will say 'I can…and I will!' Never use the word *but* as The Lessons continue! You must agree to think about and do all of the requirements and consider The Lessons to be your priority during our commitment to one another and your commitment to yourselves. As my obligation to you both, I will of course give you my best interpretation of The Lessons as I listen to what you say and as I interpret your unique situation."

The Great Wizard of The Lakes stopped talking and just looked at Gretchen and Hans. It was obviously their turn to say something.

Gretchen spoke first. "I will do all that is required in The Lessons for 'Unlocking The CAGE.' That is my commitment to myself, to Hans, and to you."

"So will I," Hans echoed as he looked first at The Great Wizard and then at Gretchen.

Even though Gretchen and Hans agreed later that they did not understand fully what The Lessons involved and certainly could not explain how they worked, The Great Wizard had offered them hope for finding an answer to their shrinking Lily Pad. They both felt that at least they had to try!

The Great Wizard drank from his Water Petal and said that The First Lesson was over. All three of them were committed to themselves and to each other, and now it was time for afternoon exercise and fun. He invited Gretchen and Hans to join him and his wife in a game of Petal Tennis before leaving. Gretchen and Hans had never played Petal Tennis before, but their instinctive athletic abilities surfaced, and everyone laughed and had a good time. Their game ended with a close score.

Hans and Gretchen swam home a little tired, but they smiled with exhilaration and happiness.

"It sure has been a different day," Hans remarked.

"Yes," Gretchen quickly responded. "Different--but fun!"

"That deserves a correction," Hans replied. "The day has been different *and* fun."

They smiled warmly at one another, hugged, turned over, and fell into a deep sleep as they floated on the quiet movements of The Lake.

COMMITMENT

THE MEMORY LEAF

1. The ingredients of success are commitment and energy.

2. There are three aspects of self:
   - what you *think*, which occurs in your head;
   - what you *feel*, which is your emotions; and
   - what you *do*, which is your self-directed behavior and actions.

3. Harmony occurs when all three aspects of self move toward the same goal. This ensures success at attaining a goal.

4. You must be committed by wanting to understand, by becoming excited about developing more awareness

and learning about yourself, and then by doing the work required in The Lessons completely.

5. You must say, "I can…*and* I will!" Avoid using the word *but*.

6. Buy a blank notebook in a design that pleases you, and use pens or pencils in colors that give you energy when you write in your notebook.
    *   Do not use your notebook and selected pens or pencils for any other purpose.
    *   Have a friend cosign and participate with you in The Lessons if you feel comfortable sharing with your friend.

7. On the first page of your notebook, write in big letters:
    *   "I CAN…AND I WILL!"
    *   Sign your name underneath the commitment.

8. On the next page, write down five of your most memorable accomplishments—things you have achieved that have given you good feelings about yourself.
    *   Trace the development of these successes so that you can visualize how much desire and energy you put into doing what was necessary in order to succeed.

- Record a descriptive mental note that what you did took work; accomplishments were not gifts.
- Write down the hurdles that you had to conquer in your journey to success.

9. Remember, you accomplished because you wanted to accomplish, and you used every force and resource available to you. You directed your energy and made things work with you and for you.

AWARENESS

THE SECOND LESSON

AWARENESS

Gretchen and Hans looked at each other and, without speaking, shared the same message: my muscles are a little sore; I'm feeling tired; and today would be such a good day to relax on The Leaf Branch near The Well of Many Spirits, especially since it looks like rain is coming.

"We made a commitment," Hans announced, "so let's do it. We can always take a day off after The Lessons end if we want to. Besides, if we don't show up, it will be very difficult to face The Great Wizard of The Lakes again—and we might need him!"

So, feeling as if they had committed to something that they were not sure they truly wanted to do, Gretchen and Hans hopped into The Lake and waved to Little Chaunce and Little Gretel as the little ones headed for the Freddies' Lily Pad. Gretchen and Hans swam away, making big, uneven ripples in The Lake that looked like shadows of their hesitant journey.

When Gretchen and Hans arrived, they realized that The Great Wizard had been up for quite a while. He had taken a morning swim and was looking out on The Lake anticipating Gretchen and Hans's arrival. He seemed eager to begin The Second Lesson.

Gretchen and Hans settled down quickly, got out their Memory Leaves and multicolored Writing Stems, and noted that The Great Wizard had placed Water Petals out for them already. The Great Wizard's commitment to Hans and Gretchen showed. He did not need any time to think, since he had already committed himself. The Great Wizard did not need to make any further choices.

"The first thing I would like you to do is write down as many things as you can remember occurring around the time you noticed that your Lily Pad was shrinking," The Great Wizard instructed.

Hans and Gretchen thought a bit and then each wrote on a Memory Leaf. When they both looked as if they had nothing else to write, The Great Wizard asked them to share their responses. Gretchen explained that she had noticed The Lily Pad starting to shrink shortly after they had invented the picnic baskets. Also, when The Warmth in The Sky shone longer and deeper, Gretchen noticed that The Lily Pad seemed smaller. She thought that maybe the heat affected the leaves. The last observation Gretchen made was that her career designing picnic baskets and cooking meals had also become hobbies and social occasions. She therefore seemed to have more company. The Freddies became like family, too. All these things had occurred during the same period of time in which she noticed that The Lily Pad was shrinking.

Hans followed with his beliefs about what had occurred. He took great pleasure in his hunting and fishing responsibilities, since it now was possible to store food in the picnic baskets. Hans noticed that The Lake seemed to be alive with goodies that season. Hans mentioned that as Little Chaunce and Little Gretel grew, he liked to be sure that they had varied special munchies and that their young lives were filled with all of the pleasures that he had had as a youngster, plus many, many more. On one festive day, he gave the little ones their own picnic baskets so that they could pick things and fill the baskets with exactly what they liked. They kept the picnic baskets next to them when they slept so that they could nibble when they awakened. Hans said that what he did to make his children happy and comfortable made him feel wonderful about himself.

Hans, unlike Gretchen, noticed the shrinking of The Lily Pad when The Warmth in The Sky was farthest away and when the nights were longest. It seemed that he worked harder during daylight to be sure there were adequate supplies for the crisp nights and ruffling winds.

Also, they created The Well of Many Spirits, where they kept grown-up drinks and snacks, soon after Gretchen had taken up a career designing picnic baskets—all at the time Hans and Gretchen started discussing the shrinking Lily Pad.

The Great Wizard seemed perplexed only for a moment. Then he knowingly said, "There are similarities and differences among what you both have noticed around the same time that your Lily Pad began to shrink. Let's not look at the specifics of what you each shared, since some of them conflict. Rather, we must look at the themes and relationships—the threads and the ribbons— that run through everything you both mentioned about different parts of your lives." The Great Wizard instructed Gretchen and Hans to look over their notes again and pick the words that frequently ran through their comments.

Gretchen and Hans read aloud, with The Great Wizard chiming in from time to time, "Picnic baskets, munchies, goodies, food storage, pleasure, love, social enjoyment, warmth, and work seasons."

Hans and Gretchen shifted positions while reaching to take sips from their Water Petals. The Great Wizard stood up a moment, stretched, and then referred to The First Lesson in which he had said that everything that occurs is related to other things—reacting to and acting toward one another. "You see," he said, "the threads of the occasions around the time when you noticed that your Lily Pad was shrinking are the threads and ribbons related to you both: your pleasures, your family, your enjoyment, your friends, your pressures, your responsibilities, The Warmth in The Sky, and The Lake. Interestingly, neither of you mentioned anything about your Lily Pad itself."

After having weaved The First Lesson into the conversation, The Great Wizard all of a sudden hopped with amazing swiftness and agility to the farthest end of his Lily Pad and then onto The Leaf Branches even farther away. This quick movement surprised Gretchen so much that the changed movement of The Lake made her drop her Writing Stem. As she tried to catch her Writing Stem, her Memory Leaves blew away. All of this happened because The Great Wizard decided to do something. Everything was related.

Then The Great Wizard of the Lakes hopped right back and landed at Hans's feet, looking him right in the eyes. Next, he hopped to the edge of his Lily Pad, jumped into The Lake, and swam away, using a swimming stroke that Gretchen and Hans had never seen before. Just as Hans and Gretchen began to wonder how far The Great Wizard would go, he suddenly turned, shot up out of The Lake, waved, splashed, and swam back with the speed of The Winged Friends of The Lake.

Gretchen and Hans were amazed to see The Great Wizard jump back on his Lily Pad, drink from his Water

Petal, and intently ask, "Where did I seem bigger than you: at your feet or when I waved from afar?"

Feeling pressed to reply, Hans said, "When you were standing right in front of me, of course."

"Look at me," The Great Wizard said sharply. "My size is constant. I have not changed. I was the same size at your feet, at the edge of my Lily Pad, and far away in The Lake. Your size is constant, too!" The Great Wizard paused and looked as if he was studying the thoughts of both Gretchen and Hans. After a few pensive moments, he went on. "Your position, your vantage point relative to mine, and your perceptions are responsible for making you think of me as bigger or smaller. If you, Hans, felt taller than me, then even if I stood in front of you, I would appear smaller than you. I would appear smaller still from a distance. Size is a concept that requires a comparison. Nobody and nothing is 'bigger than or smaller than' unless compared with somebody or something else. It is also impossible to be better, different, or worse than something or someone else without comparison!"

The Great Wizard's voice grew deeper, as if he was about to say something even more important. "You know my real size. So, when you think of me close, you choose to see me bigger because I occupy most of the area that you can see. When you focus on a bigger stretch of The Lake, you see me smaller. You must always remember that you are in control of what you see."

Hans's and Gretchen's eyes began to widen, perhaps because each had questions, or they felt perplexed, or maybe they were becoming aware. They seemed unable to speak, and The Great Wizard sat with them in silence a few moments.

"The Second Lesson," The Great Wizard said finally, in a deep, comforting voice that reflected the emotion in the moment, "is the premise that *all of us are exactly what we want to be*, and *all of us see what is in focus,* with respect to our resources and surroundings. When I wanted to seem bigger, I stood near you; when I wanted to seem smaller, I jumped away from you. The need, then, is to become aware of what we are and what we can do to be perceived differently. Only when we look at ourselves, truly feel our emotions, and accept ourselves, can we direct our behavior toward becoming what we want to be, toward creating another realistic image and putting all aspects of ourselves—thoughts, emotions, and actions—into meeting our new goal."

Gretchen and Hans seemed to have little to say and, at the same time, looked as though they had some understanding. The atmosphere was quiet, and both Gretchen's and Hans's thoughts were dancing with emotional electricity that bounced off every movement and every word, trying to connect into an understood pattern.

Drinking the last from his Water Petal, The Great Wizard said he had an assignment for Hans and Gretchen to do that evening. He asked them to go to the edge of their Lily Pad before The Warmth in The Sky left, and to look into The Lake Mirror. "Study your reflections… think…and study your thoughts," The Great Wizard advised. "Then ask yourself, 'Is this the way I want to be?' If it is, then great; enjoy yourself and redesign your space on your shrinking Lily Pad. However, if the image that you see and think about in your reflections is not how you want to be and feel, both realistically and optimally, then tell yourself out loud: 'This is not the way that I want to be!' Step back, close your eyes, stretch, and take a deep breath. As you reflect on The Lake and the images that you see, think about all of the things that you remember occurring when you also started believing that your Lily Pad was shrinking."

The Great Wizard further instructed Gretchen and Hans that after getting up from The Dinner Leaf and helping Little Chaunce and Little Gretel go to sleep that night, they should fill their Water Petals and go to a new space on their Lily Pad. "Think again about what you noticed in The Lake Mirror—both the ribbons and the threads. Create mental Snapshots of your reflections. For example, think about the picnic baskets, social enjoyment, munchies, and The Well of Many Spirits. Then look at yourselves, study what you see, and think about the aspects of each ribbon that make you each feel good and in control. Also, consider the same ribbons, and try to discover what you don't like about them—what makes you uncomfortable and feel out of control. Make mental pictures—Snapshots—of all that you see."

The Great Wizard of The Lakes instructed Gretchen and Hans to make notes using their special Writing Stems and Memory Leaves to spark their memories and to stay aware of their perceptions. Further, he told them to go over the mental Snapshots as often as possible. "Always allow enough time to give everything careful, unrushed consideration," he urged.

The Great Wizard indicated that The Third Lesson would be the key for discerning how Gretchen and Hans imagined they would like to feel on their Lily Pad. "There might be new beginnings," The Great Wizard pointed out. He encouraged Hans and Gretchen to keep their thoughts and discoveries fresh in their minds. "Think, feel, talk about, and write down on your Memory Leaves what you become aware of during this evening—as much and as often as possible."

As The Great Wizard waved good-bye, he told Hans and Gretchen to say to each other and to think about, over and over again:

I put on the eyeglasses
That give me the image
That I want to see.

I hold the power to become
Whatever
I want to be.

I alone am responsible!

It was a thought-filled evening. Little Chaunce and Little Gretel responded to their parents' pensive moods, and all seemed to eat more as they struggled to fill the silence over The Dinner Leaf. Hugs and kisses were quiet and strong, and the little ones scurried off to bed without a fuss, holding onto their picnic baskets more tightly than usual.

Hans and Gretchen completed their assignments and spoke little of other things. They went to bed early, too. Their changing moods echoed as a soft mist fell on every crevice of their world…even in their recurring dream.

THE DREAM

I am what I want to be.
I must want to be what I am.

Since I want to be what I am,
I can want to be what I am not.

If I am not what I want to be,
I can become what I am not.

Because
I am what I want to be.

$\mathscr{A}$ WARENESS

$\mathscr{T}$HE MEMORY LEAF

1. A commitment leaves no outs. When you decide to do something, the time to begin is when you decide—the clock starts at that moment—for there is no better time.

    - The time to end whatever commitment you make is only when your goal is reached. Some commitments are forever.
    - Do not break a contract with yourself! Treat your contract with yourself as if it were a legal document. Do not attempt to convince yourself that it does not matter if you break a contract with yourself since no one else is involved. You count the most!

2. Do not let a passing moment of doubt interfere with your carefully planned dreams. Dreams live after

doubts are dismissed. Dreams move you forward; doubts move you backward. Life is never still. It either flows forward or flows backward. You choose its direction.

- Always direct yourself toward a better today and tomorrow.
- Consider what can happen each day, and prepare to stay aimed on your goals.
- Put all forces to work for yourself—be sure to take your best efforts at whatever you set out to do.

3. Look into a mirror and write down the circumstances that stand out in your life. What are the threads and ribbons that follow along on your individual journey?

- Have you always felt overweight?
- Do you think that you drink too much?
- Do you say that you are addicted to cigarettes?
- Are there happy things in your life that you often think about and feel?
- Do you overeat when stressed?
- Are you short-tempered at certain times or under certain conditions?
- Are any relationships lacking positive energy?
- Do you wish that you could do something but never get there?

4. Think about the threads and ribbons through two lenses.
    - What about each ribbon makes you feel satisfied and in control?
    - Describe how each ribbon may make you feel unhappy and either out of control or at a loss of self-control.

5. Ribbons are unique to your individual world. Their size is an interpretation of what you see and feel against the backdrop on which they are portrayed.
    - If you feel mostly in control of the majority of your ribbons, the few "less controllable ribbons" do not look as big.
    - If you have big areas that make you unhappy, however, and you feel helpless to control them, these may be consuming most of the space in your unique picture.

6. Think…feel…talk…and write about what you have uncovered.
    - Review your thoughts frequently.
    - Create mental Snapshots of your thoughts.
    - Take the time to consider your thoughts and Snapshots carefully.

7. Say to yourself over and over again:

> I choose the eyeglasses
> That give me the image
> That I want to see.
>
> I have the power to become
> Whatever
> I want to be.
>
> I alone am responsible!

GOALS

$\mathcal{T}$HE THIRD LESSON

$\mathcal{G}$OALS

$\mathbf{E}$arly morning activities got caught in the whirlwind of anticipation that Gretchen and Hans shared on this new day. Of all The Lessons, Gretchen and Hans both believed that this one would hold the form for making their feelings live and breathe—give them the brushes and paint for their unique pictures—and give them the knowledge and answers for creating the Life Designs that matched their Snapshots.

The swim seemed shorter as the yellow reflections of The Warmth in the Sky cast a guiding glow in the direction of The Lily Pad of The Great Wizard of The Lakes. It was as if The Lake had formed a cushion around Gretchen and Hans, softening their long journey.

Instead of throwing just one flower to signal their request to visit, Hans and Gretchen each tossed a flower onto The Lily Pad. The Great Wizard of The Lakes received them with a sparkle of warmth and full understanding of the unspoken message. Hans and Gretchen could feel and almost embrace the energy in the air.

Gretchen, Hans, and The Great Wizard settled down quickly, snuggling into comfortable positions. "*Think, feel, and do,*" The Great Wizard began. "Living together, these activities are the keys for 'Unlocking Your CAGE.'"

The Great Wizard asked Gretchen and Hans to relax further by curling into their spaces and closing their eyes. After instructing Hans and Gretchen to take a few comforting, deep breaths, The Great Wizard carried them away from the realities of the moment to what he called The New Place. He explained that The New Place was a world where Gretchen and Hans immediately appeared stronger and more self-assured, bubbling with energy. The Sky was transparent and blue, and a few puffy pieces of cotton floated across the horizon, adding dimension to the picture rather than being intrusive. It was beautiful most of the time in The New Place, because whatever Gretchen and Hans chose to look at always had two surfaces—the smooth and beautiful, and the rough and bumpy. They were advised to view both surfaces and then to focus on the beautiful surface, even though they occasionally noticed or thought about the bumps. "Direct what you think and see," The Great Wizard coached them, "as if you were focusing a camera."

The Great Wizard continued to speak. "The Earth is dark, unknown, and hard. It is also strong and sturdy—supporting us with conviction and security. The Snow is biting and cold, yet it melts on our faces and makes us glow warmly with its sting. The Night is empty, cold, and dark, moving us to cuddle for warmth around The Nest of Heat. The Nest of Heat can destroy; it can also be used to save and to restore."

The scene changed as Hans and Gretchen remained cozily curled together with their eyes closed, enveloped with sounds and images. "Everything around you in The New Place must be thought of as *perfect*," The Great Wizard announced, "for everything is doing its best, given its unique situation and the unique attributes it has been given on its journey of living. Considering what is *perfect* is the best that is possible for any particular moment. Things may be different later, and when the best is given again, it also is *perfect* at that time."

Gretchen blinked a little, and though Hans's eyes remained closed, The Great Wizard responded to a question in his thoughts. "Let me give you some examples," The Great Wizard said. "One tree, growing in response to the meadow, stands tall and straight in wide spaces and on the flat ground. Another tree grows between rock formations, reaching at angles for The Warmth in The Sky. Still another, deprived of water in its early years, forever bears the bite of starvation in its trunk. Because of the oppressed angles of its growth, this tree catches the twinkling of color-sparked mist as it reflects The Warmth in The Sky created by the beams of Father Sun. No other tree comes close to generating so much echoing beauty." In a deepening voice that filled The Water Universe, The Great Wizard added, "All of the trees are *perfect* in The New Place. They have taken what has been given, what is, and have grown the best way that they considered to be possible."

With the mood unbroken and after a moment of silence, The Great Wizard asked Gretchen and Hans to recall their Snapshots and thoughts viewed through The Lake Mirror the evening before. "Look at the ribbons and threads that make you feel good and in control. In contrast, think about those aspects that make you feel uncomfortable—out of control or unhappy. Bring them into The New Place—The Perfect New Place where you have the power to create, to see, and to change whatever you desire. With your eyes still closed, imagine your Snapshots here. Make them alive. Now, think about what you feel. Feel the emotions. Remember the Snapshots that bring you joy and feelings of success. Study your achievements as you stroll through The Perfect New Place looking at the scenery of possibilities. Then look at the ribbons and threads that make you unhappy. Also remember, everything in The Perfect New Place is scenery. You are the heart and the pulse giving The New Place life. *You* control The Perfect New Place by extending your thoughts and excitement into your *behavior*. You move your own camera lenses around. You can make what you like bigger or you can change what you do not like by making it smaller. Do what you think and feel! Everything will respond to your direction, your behavior."

Hans, Gretchen, and The Great Wizard stretched, awakening in the present.

Gretchen observed that she felt as if she were wrapped in velvet.

The Great Wizard drank from his Water Petal, as though quenching a thirst, yet he seemed eager to continue. "I want you to think intently about Your Perfect New Place at least four times a day and always before you begin the day and before you end the evening. As you awaken, begin dreaming, and then dream as you go to sleep. Always end your dreams with a vivid image of your Snapshots. Study how you feel, decide how you want to feel, think about how you behave, decide how you want to behave, and know that your dreams are real. They may become your goals if that is your desire."

"You came here," The Great Wizard went on, "because of discomfort with your feeling that your Lily Pad was shrinking. Looking at the ribbons and threads of your unique lives, how will you behave so that you will be what you want to be? What should you do? How can you change your perception that your Lily Pad is shrinking?"

Hans's and Gretchen's eyes widened; they were ready to receive—to be told.

The Great Wizard stood, elevating his presence and size and making his authority more pronounced.

"*You have all the answers,*" The Great Wizard declared, studying Gretchen and Hans in turn. "You do not need me or anyone else to tell you how to behave, what to eat, what to keep in your picnic basket, what to serve around The Dinner Leaf, how to celebrate Great Harvest Day, how to welcome and embrace family and friends, how to enjoy quiet time, how to share with those you love, and what to give Little Chaunce and Little Gretel in their picnic baskets."

The Great Wizard sat down after a pause, positioning himself closely between Hans and Gretchen and building a circle of intimacy. Then The Great Wizard continued. "Whatever I know, you know. You have all the power there is. You paint your own pictures, given your unique gifts. No one in the Water Universe has more potent understanding of your talents than yourself. Unlock your knowledge and energy, and use it to become whatever you want to be!"

The Great Wizard's words felt as sharp and precise to Gretchen and Hans as finely edged crystal. They both swallowed slowly, as if to taste, savor, and accept what felt like the ultimate challenge.

Now the voice of The Great Wizard became even more vibrant and determined. "Before you act, PAUSE for a moment while bringing your Snapshots into view. ASK yourself, 'Is what I am planning to do going to support my journey toward my goals?' If it is, fine. Then consciously DECIDE to PROCEED with the behavior. If it is not, then ASK yourself, 'Is what I am planning more important than my goals?' If you answer 'no,' then create alternative behaviors that uphold your goals. Use each other for ideas—call on friends—ask for help if necessary. However, if you answer, 'Yes, my goal is not important right now,' then before you do anything, drink a full Water Petal, move to a different Leaf Branch, and PAUSE to study your thoughts in front of the Lake Mirror. Take the conscious time to do all of this before you DECIDE to PROCEED with breaking the commitment to yourself. Concentrate on your Snapshots before you DECIDE anything. If you stumble off your goal, get back on it as soon as possible, just as Gretchen got back on The Lily Pad when she had to fetch Little Chaunce because he had lost his balance and fallen into The Lake."

It seemed like a long Lesson to Gretchen and Hans, but The Great Wizard was still sharing. "Everything in The Third Lesson is grounded on the assumption that you know what makes you feel good and in control. You know what you want to change—what makes you uncomfortable and feeling out of control. You can pick your own goals, one or two at a time." The Great Wizard continued, "You know what behaviors are contrary to your goals. You know what makes you feel big and strong. You know what makes you feel small and powerless. Do not delude yourself and do something 'just once,' or 'just today,' or say, 'tomorrow I will start again.' If you do, what you are really saying is 'my dreams are not important,' 'my commitment to myself does not matter,' and 'I would rather think that The Lily Pad is shrinking than have The Perfect New Place be my only home.' "

"Always remember," The Great Wizard added quickly, "only this moment counts. Nothing else lives, so make each and every decision move you forward. Think only about times that you stumble in order to become aware and to learn. Think about your successful behaviors in order to reward yourself for what you did to feel good; then use the moment to go forward again. Your Perfect New Place lives now. Now…is…all…there…is…. *Now* shares its place with nothing else. This moment must count!"

The Great Wizard paused between words, emphasizing each one. Then he seemed to move back from the intensity and the awakening push of The Third Lesson.

Quickly and with the sigh that follows being full, Gretchen and Hans mirrored the motions of The Great Wizard of The Lakes and sat back.

Gretchen and Hans both felt drained of energy. The Great Wizard acknowledged that they were tired as he instructed them to go home and to think about The Third Lesson. "As often as possible, bring your Snapshots into

Your Perfect New Place. Know that you have everything necessary to make your dreams live. Your dreams may not live exactly as you expect, but they will live. And, the more energy you give your dreams, the more powerful they will become." The Great Wizard's parting counsel was for Gretchen and Hans to corner every spare minute to think about their Perfect New Place, to feel its wonder, and to rehearse those behaviors that would give life to their dreams.

Then, recognizing the exhaustion that follows intense concentration, The Great Wizard promised that The Fourth Lesson would be easier. He said it would involve scenery—the light and the shadows—the often elusive qualities that either define or mute a picture.

It was a quiet swim home. Upon their arrival, Hans and Gretchen noticed that the Freddies were sitting with Little Gretel and Little Chaunce around The Family Gathering Leaf. Little Chaunce and Little Gretel clutched their picnic baskets. Gretchen and Hans were fatigued. The Freddies immediately got up and said that they did not want to intrude and needed to leave. They had only wanted to keep Little Chaunce and Little Gretel from feeling lonely. Gretchen and Hans said nothing, but their expressions indicated how grateful they were to their loved friends and for the sensitivity of understanding that emanated from them in that moment.

The family completed the necessary chores. They exchanged hugs and kisses. Dreams melted into every space. Gretchen and Hans fell into deep sleep. It was one of the few times that both Gretchen and Hans did not seem to need to sit on The Leaf Branch sipping from The Well of Many Spirits before bedtime.

$\mathscr{G}$ O A L

$\mathscr{T}$ HE MEMORY LEAF

1. The keys for being the way you want to be are thinking, feeling, and doing.
   - These keys must be in agreement with one another, and all or as much as possible of their energy must flow toward your goals.

2. Perfection is doing the best with your unique talents and attributes at any given moment in time.
   - Study yourself realistically and love the moment when you use the best of what you have been given—that is when you have been perfect!
   - Tomorrow you may do things differently. Just remember that if you do your best tomorrow also, both yesterday and today have been perfect.

3. Take yourself away from the present.
    -   Close your eyes, stretch, relax, and take a few long, deep breaths.
    -   Think about a place of great comfort to you, a place where you feel self-assured, strong, and fulfilled, where life dances happily around you, and where you feel your best.
    -   This comforting place may be somewhere you have been before—having felt mostly good things—or it may be some place that you wish to go.
    -   Think of the place that you chose as Your Perfect New Place.

4. Once you have walked through Your Perfect New Place, recall your dreams and Snapshots—that is, what makes you feel good and successful. Also, recall what makes you uncomfortable, helpless, or feel out of control.
    -   Walk through Your Perfect New Place feeling the wonder, the pride, and the love for yourself.
    -   Hold closely Your Perfect New Place and your Snapshots. Remember that everything is your creation.

5. At least four times a day, and always before getting out of bed in the morning and before going to sleep at night, take yourself to Your Perfect New Place and be as you are in your Snapshots.
    - Feel your dreams, think about them, and then behave and act the rest of the day in ways that make dreams that you desire—your goals—closer to reality.
    - Make your goals happen. They will be real when you *will* them to live. Think them, feel them, and do things that move you toward success and away from discomfort.

6. *You* know all of the answers for creating Your Perfect New Place.
    - *You* know what will help you to get there and what will move you away from your goal.
    - No one knows anything better or more than *you*.

7. Before you do anything,
    - PAUSE a moment while thinking of your Snapshots—your goals.
    - ASK yourself, "Is what I am planning to do going to support my journey toward my goals?" Keep your Snapshots in mind.

8. If "Yes" is your answer,
    - DECIDE to
    - PROCEED with your intended behaviors.

9. If "No" is your answer,
    - ASK yourself, "Is what I am planning more important than my goals?"
      If you answer "No," then create alternatives that follow your goals.
    - Call on friends, or ask someone for help, if necessary.

10. If your answer is "Yes—what I am planning right now is more important than my goals," then…
    - drink a glass of water and
    - occupy yourself with another thought or activity for at least one minute before you
    - DECIDE to PROCEED with the unhelpful behavior.
    - BE SURE TO CONCENTRATE ON YOUR SNAPSHOTS BEFORE YOU DECIDE TO ABANDON YOUR GOALS!

11. If you did something that was not helpful toward your goals, admit that *you* chose to do it, study what happened, and learn from it. Then, move forward in a way that respects your renewed commitment

to yourself, to your goals, and to the contract with yourself.

- You are the most important person and friend to yourself.

12. Remember, this moment is all that counts! It is *now*. Consciously use the moment so that you can feel perfect within yourself, for yourself.

- Do not delude yourself by saying you will do something "just once," "just today," or you will "start after the weekend."
- Make each and every decision count so that you always move forward.
- The most important responsibility that you have to yourself is to live in the *now*! No other time exists.

EXERCISE

THE FOURTH LESSON

EXERCISE

The Warmth in The Sky gave its shining glow to The Lake early—catching Gretchen and Hans with a quick and bubbly awakening. As they looked up, even The Winged Friends of The Lake seemed to move with greater determination and energy toward their destinations. The Lake danced.

By the time Little Gretel and Little Chaunce arrived at The Family Gathering Leaf, Gretchen had already finished her chores and arranged the berries Hans had cheerfully picked that morning. The berries had eye-catching and mouth-watering appeal because they were fresh and picked with love; everyone ate heartily and then cleared The Leaf together.

It was still too early to leave to see The Great Wizard, so Hans asked Gretchen if she would like to swim over to The Growing Pond to see his thriving Food Beds. Off they went as Little Chaunce and Little Gretel swam in the opposite direction to The Learning Garden. It was a particularly good season, so the specialty plants in The Food Beds seemed to smile in perkiness and fullness as they watched The Warmth in The Sky. Since Gretchen and Hans swam with The Warmth in The Sky behind them, it looked as if The Growing Pond's Food Beds were standing to welcome their visitors.

Gretchen and Hans paddled through The Growing Pond and quietly shared the thought that The Growing Pond felt like Their Perfect New Place. They had created The Growing Pond by using the gifts from The Lakes and The Warmth in The Sky. In addition, it took great diligence and energy to keep The Growing Pond beautiful.

After looking at and touching the natural wonders on and near The Growing Pond as well as picking a basketful of naturally sweet berries, Gretchen and Hans decided to leave to see The Great Wizard for The Fourth Lesson. Their dreams and Snapshots were fresh and alive in their minds. The Lake seemed to flow in the direction they were taking. It felt like a beautiful new day.

Hans and Gretchen embellished the usual welcome from The Great Wizard with a gift of fresh berries from their Growing Pond, placed in a newly designed picnic basket. The Great Wizard immediately set the basket out in the middle of the Water Petals and encouraged Gretchen and Hans to share his gift. He complimented Gretchen on the picnic basket and told Hans that the berries were superb. "Would you share what you do to make these berries seem to burst with flavor?" The Great Wizard asked. "I would love to learn your special growing techniques."

Hans assured The Great Wizard that he would share all of his talents.

The casualness and calm of the day seemed to melt through The Fourth Lesson. An air of serenity, wisdom, and alertness haloed the picture. The beginning of a new pathway to Life's Journey seemed to excite both Hans and Gretchen.

"You see," The Great Wizard said, "you are in 'Your CAGE' if you believe that outside forces control you, that your Lily Pad is shrinking, that you are helpless to stop the process, that you are a victim of The Forces, or that answers are outside yourselves. 'Unlocking Your CAGE' means that through your Commitment, Awareness, Goals, and The Fourth Lesson—Exercise, you control yourselves: your ribbons and threads, and what you see, feel, and find. Of course, there are things in reality around you that you must consider as you set your goals. Given what is, however, *you* unlock the power of your thoughts and emotions and harness their energies into behaviors that you direct. You shape your dreams and Snapshots by using the gifts and talents that you hold and by using the positive forces in every happening."

Now The Great Wizard's voice deepened. "Actually, there is no 'CAGE.' Your CAGE exists only if you give it life by feeling CAGED—by being unaware and uncommitted and by feeling unable to control yourself. *You* direct what you believe to exist. If your CAGE is not real in your mind because it has been unlocked, then it simply does not live; it cannot be. And that knowledge frees you to know that what you believe *is* real and *does* exist. It means that you can take the positive aspects of your journey and make them bigger. It means that you can take not-so-positive things and make them smaller. And if you make one thing bigger, the other thing next to it seems smaller. You control the picture—what you think, what you feel, and what you do!"

The Great Wizard dipped into the picnic basket and grabbed a berry as he shifted his position. "That brings me to The Fourth and final Lesson: Exercise. Exercise occurs on two surfaces. You exercise your mind by thinking about and by feeling the excitements of Your Perfect New Place; you exercise your body by behaving in ways that take you to Your Perfect New Place—so that your journey feels comfortable. Exercise means using your mind and your body to their fullest capacities. It means striving to think about your dreams, looking at your Snapshots, and then doing everything possible to move toward your goals—using your resources and strengths to their fullest—putting every positive force available to work for and with you. Further, exercise means enjoying your gifts and talents. It means creating ways to blend with friends and family, in private and social moments, in ways that feel good. Playing, painting designs, gardening, learning, and laughing: these are all examples of exercise."

The Great Wizard rose and, with exceptional clarity, showed a change in mood. "Let's take a swim. I'd like to teach you a new water movement that I learned at Swimming Camp—it's really fast and graceful."

By the time The Great Wizard, Hans, Gretchen, and The Great Wizard's wife, who joined them on The Lake, were finished, The Warmth in The Sky was directly overhead, shining down in long yellow streams of connection. Climbing onto The Lily Pad, Gretchen noted with the glee of accomplishment how easy it had been for her to catch on to the new swimming movement. Hans observed that she always had a talent for swimming; all she had to do was to risk stretching her talent in an unknown or a different direction. "The ease of learning the new swimming movement may have been a surprise to you," Hans said, "but I knew that you would learn it—fast!"

The Great Wizard smiled warmly and shared more as the ribbons from The Warmth in The Sky dried him off. "The greatest contrast you must build into Your Perfect New Place is mental exercise and physical exercise." The Great Wizard drank from his Water Petal and nibbled on some berries. Then he added, "The Warmth in The Sky seems warmer after a cool swim. The Lake is refreshing after sitting directly under The Warmth in The Sky. In order to feel The Warmth in The Sky fully, you must first leave it and then return and study your feelings. Mental exercise and physical exercise are our natural, innate gifts and talents. Through each day, both must exist in separate dances in order for each to exist in our minds and be noticed fully for all that they have to offer."

Gretchen and Hans felt sad to leave The Great Wizard. The picnic basket holding the morning's berries had been their gift to him, and they both knew that The Great Wizard's Lessons were free. Gretchen was just so proud of her career in designing picnic baskets, as was Hans of his successes in The Growing Pond, that it seemed natural to share their happiness with The Great Wizard.

Using their newly learned swimming movements to swim away from The Lily Pad of The Great Wizard of The Lakes, Hans and Gretchen turned back and waved from a distance. Though the Great Wizard and his big smile were far away from Gretchen and Hans, he felt very close. Gretchen and Hans both knew that even though they were leaving The Great Wizard, he would always be with them. His Lessons lived in many places, on many surfaces of their lives, and would continue to teach them and to frame their world over time.

The Great Wizard, smiling but sad, stood on the edge of his Lily Pad. He had given all of his best Lessons, and he knew that only by giving them away could they truly be his forever. He also knew that everything he had tried to teach Hans and Gretchen, they already knew. Somehow, the scene had become cloudy, but just for a time. The Great Wizard of The Lakes waved good-bye as he thought, "Maybe they will need me again; maybe they won't. Maybe I'll see them again; maybe I won't."

EXERCISE

THE MEMORY LEAF

1. You are CAGED if you believe that outside forces
    control you.
    *   You can feel free and in control through
        Commitment,
        Awareness,
        Goals, and
        Exercise.
    *   These four factors *Unlock Your CAGE.*

2. In truth, your CAGE does not exist unless you give it
    life.
    *   You direct what you believe to exist.
    *   You control your picture—
        What you think,
        What you feel, and
        What you do!

- You put on the eyeglasses that give you the images that you choose to see!

3. Mental exercise and physical exercise are your own best natural and innate contrasts. When one is in focus, the other lives in its background—like a frame and a canvas. The more that you focus on or exercise one, the clearer and stronger the other becomes when you look at it. Stepping away from thinking, feeling, and doing and moving to pure physical exercise give more strength to the mental exercises when you return to them.
   - Total involvement with one precludes the other, freeing you to experience your distinct energies.
   - Throughout each day, both physical and mental exercise must exist in order for each to exist, to be felt fully, and to be as deep and focused as you desire.

4. Select one or two physical activities—talents, capabilities, physical likes, or just desires—or simply select something that you would like to learn or to try.
   - Design a program for yourself based on your selections.
   - Enroll yourself in the program—in a formal contract or course, or in an informal contract with yourself or with a friend.

- Follow your program's design and make it an integral part of your daily activities.
- Do not break a contract with yourself!

5. At least once every day, before or after physical activity, spend time thinking about what you feel and your activity.
   - Renew your commitment to yourself.
   - Search for new understanding of an existing behavior that you may wish to change.
   - Analyze what you did and why you did it.
   - Change what you do and the way that you do it if you think it best.
   - Underscore or reset your goals.
   - Keep exercising your mind and body so that you feel energy.

6. At least once a week, and whenever you desire or feel the need, reread The Lessons and your notebook.'
   - Share your experiences with friends if you feel comfortable doing so.

Several years later…

It was Graduation Day on The Lake. Gretel was to receive a Star Flower for her accomplishments in Figure Leaf Hopping, a form of gymnastics. Chaunce, a rather pensive opposite compared with his sister, was to be awarded a Star Flower for his artistic rendition of "The Great Harvest Leaf."

The day bubbled with energy, as evidenced by the smiles and hugs. Gretchen and Hans awoke early, as usual, and busied themselves with preparations for The Great Festive Day, always an anthem of Graduation Day and filled with various activities. The Freddies were expected, of course, since they were considered family. Hans and Gretchen had also invited many other friends to drop by.

Hans took Gretchen's largest picnic basket and swam off to The Growing Pond to pick the fresh berries and other delicacies he had cultivated with passion, precision, and pride. Gretchen used that time to arrange The Lily Pad so that guests could sit and move around comfortably.

Her newly acquired skills in Interior Lily Pad Designing gave her various ideas. It seemed as though she was always creating excitement by changing The Lily Pad around. It was amazing what she could do with space. Gretchen actually credited Hans's arrangement of The Growing Pond with some of her ideas. Hans, however, said that he had caught Gretchen's creativity, and that is why he had become known as The Gardening Wizard of The Lakes. Their accomplishments seemed to be their dance.

Gretel used the time before guests arrived to practice her figures so that she could share with family and friends the Leaf Hops that had won her the enviable prize. She loved to hear others say, "You're in such great shape! How do you do it?" This was the ultimate compliment. She always identified and then accentuated her assets.

Thoughtful Chaunce gave gentle directions to everybody—to Hans on the foods to grow and pick, to Gretchen on how best to serve so that guests were fed evenly throughout the day, and to Gretel on how to receive compliments graciously. Sometimes Chaunce acted as if he wanted to become the next Great Wizard.

It was a Perfect Day. Everyone shared his or her best, and the day was a blend of what people gave to one another—ideas, dreams, accomplishments, goals, and beliefs. One playful sharing exercise of the day was for everyone at The Great Festive Day celebration to share what they believed to be his or her unique gift. While most seemed to savor the moment of personally sharing something special about themselves, some had a hard time discovering their unique talents. However, they were encouraged and received help, and they finally found their gifts and were able to describe them to all listeners.

For The Great Festive Day, many of those present offered specialties that they had personally created, grown, picked, or arranged. Each offering was healthful and natural, reflecting the symbolic picture given by Chaunce. Throughout the day food became an energizing accompaniment to the focal point of festive activities and sharing. Full and sparkling Water Petals appeared everywhere; those who needed a tiny confection could always dip into The Floating Flower Tulips filled with sugarcane gumdrops, a natural variety of the sweet. Hans had cultivated The Floating Flower Tulips to replace The Well of Many Spirits. Everything present allowed family and guests to paint their pictures of love, warmth, fullness, and security.

Everyone believed that it was a truly Perfect Day that each personally created.

Later that evening, after all the guests had left, Gretchen and Hans decided to relax in the cooling waters before going to sleep. They were still happy with energy. They smiled at one another as they swam around the stillness of The Lake, only lightly moving the water.

Chaunce and Gretel were on the other side of The Lake swimming around the Water Bushes, trying to decide where to plant their Star Flowers for The Water Universe to enjoy—for the ages to come. Soon they all gathered on The Lily Pad, shared reactions to the wonderful day, hugged, expressed good wishes for all of the graduates and Lake Friends, and went to sleep.

Startled, Hans awoke in the middle of the night. He had had a phenomenal dream and had to write down its essence before its clarity was lost in the mist of his subconscious. Reaching in the dark for the Writing Stem and Memory Leaf that he always kept close, Hans scribbled what he remembered and then drifted back into the Land of Dreams.

In the morning, as The Warmth in The Sky gently widened his eyes and opened his thoughts, he yawned, stretched, and read:

Once upon a time…

They decided they would
   They discovered they could
     And
       They did!

         Again…

    And again…

            And again….

    Occasionally, they stumbled…

      Once in a while, they asked for help….

The End

and then…

The Beginning…

MEMORY LEAF APPENDIX

COMMITMENT

THE MEMORY LEAF

1. The ingredients of success are commitment and energy.

2. There are three aspects of self:
    - what you *think*, which occurs in your head;
    - what you *feel*, which is your emotions; and
    - what you *do*, which is your self-directed behavior and actions.

3. Harmony occurs when all three aspects of self move toward the same goal. This ensures success at attaining a goal.

4. You must be committed by wanting to understand, by becoming excited about developing more awareness

and learning about yourself, and then by doing the work required in The Lessons completely.

5. You must say, "I can…*and* I will!" Avoid using the word *but*.

6. Buy a blank notebook in a design that pleases you, and use pens or pencils in colors that give you energy when you write in your notebook.
    *   Do not use your notebook and selected pens or pencils for any other purpose.
    *   Have a friend cosign and participate with you in The Lessons if you feel comfortable sharing with your friend.

7. On the first page of your notebook, write in big letters:
    *   "I CAN…AND I WILL!"
    *   Sign your name underneath the commitment.

8. On the next page, write down five of your most memorable accomplishments—things you have achieved that have given you good feelings about yourself.
    *   Trace the development of these successes so that you can visualize how much desire and energy you put into doing what was necessary in order to succeed.

- Record a descriptive mental note that what you did took work; accomplishments were not gifts.
- Write down the hurdles that you had to conquer in your journey to success.

9. Remember, you accomplished because you wanted to accomplish, and you used every force and resource available to you. You directed your energy and made things work with you and for you.

$\mathcal{A}$WARENESS

$\mathcal{T}$HE MEMORY LEAF

1. A commitment leaves no outs. When you decide to do something, the time to begin is when you decide— the clock starts at that moment—for there is no better time.

    - The time to end whatever commitment you make is only when your goal is reached. Some commitments are forever.
    - Do not break a contract with yourself! Treat your contract with yourself as if it were a legal document. Do not attempt to convince yourself that it does not matter if you break a contract with yourself since no one else is involved. You count the most!

2. Do not let a passing moment of doubt interfere with your carefully planned dreams. Dreams live after

doubts are dismissed. Dreams move you forward; doubts move you backward. Life is never still. It either flows forward or flows backward. You choose its direction.

- Always direct yourself toward a better today and tomorrow.
- Consider what can happen each day, and prepare to stay aimed on your goals.
- Put all forces to work for yourself—be sure to take your best efforts at whatever you set out to do.

3. Look into a mirror and write down the circumstances that stand out in your life. What are the threads and ribbons that follow along on your individual journey?
    - Have you always felt overweight?
    - Do you think that you drink too much?
    - Do you say that you are addicted to cigarettes?
    - Are there happy things in your life that you often think about and feel?
    - Do you overeat when stressed?
    - Are you short-tempered at certain times or under certain conditions?
    - Are any relationships lacking positive energy?
    - Do you wish that you could do something but never get there?

4. Think about the threads and ribbons through two lenses.
    - What about each ribbon makes you feel satisfied and in control?
    - Describe how each ribbon may make you feel unhappy and either out of control or at a loss of self-control.

5. Ribbons are unique to your individual world. Their size is an interpretation of what you see and feel against the backdrop on which they are portrayed.
    - If you feel mostly in control of the majority of your ribbons, the few "less controllable ribbons" do not look as big.
    - If you have big areas that make you unhappy, however, and you feel helpless to control them, these may be consuming most of the space in your unique picture.

6. Think…feel…talk…and write about what you have uncovered.
    - Review your thoughts frequently.
    - Create mental Snapshots of your thoughts.
    - Take the time to consider your thoughts and Snapshots carefully.

7.   Say to yourself over and over again:

> I choose the eyeglasses
> That give me the image
> That I want to see.
>
> I have the power to become
> Whatever
> I want to be.
>
> I alone am responsible!

GOAL

THE MEMORY LEAF

1. The keys for being the way you want to be are thinking, feeling, and doing.
   - These keys must be in agreement with one another, and all or as much as possible of their energy must flow toward your goals.

2. Perfection is doing the best with your unique talents and attributes at any given moment in time.
   - Study yourself realistically and love the moment when you use the best of what you have been given—that is when you have been perfect!
   - Tomorrow you may do things differently. Just remember that if you do your best tomorrow also, both yesterday and today have been perfect.

3. Take yourself away from the present.
    -   Close your eyes, stretch, relax, and take a few long, deep breaths.
    -   Think about a place of great comfort to you, a place where you feel self-assured, strong, and fulfilled, where life dances happily around you, and where you feel your best.
    -   This comforting place may be somewhere you have been before—having felt mostly good things—or it may be some place that you wish to go.
    -   Think of the place that you chose as Your Perfect New Place.

4. Once you have walked through Your Perfect New Place, recall your dreams and Snapshots—that is, what makes you feel good and successful. Also, recall what makes you uncomfortable, helpless, or feel out of control.
    -   Walk through Your Perfect New Place feeling the wonder, the pride, and the love for yourself.
    -   Hold closely Your Perfect New Place and your Snapshots. Remember that everything is your creation.

5. At least four times a day, and always before getting out of bed in the morning and before going to sleep at night, take yourself to Your Perfect New Place and be as you are in your Snapshots.

    *   Feel your dreams, think about them, and then behave and act the rest of the day in ways that make dreams that you desire—your goals— closer to reality.
    *   Make your goals happen. They will be real when you *will* them to live. Think them, feel them, and do things that move you toward success and away from discomfort.

6. *You* know all of the answers for creating Your Perfect New Place.

    *   *You* know what will help you to get there and what will move you away from your goal.
    *   No one knows anything better or more than *you*.

7. Before you do anything,

    *   PAUSE a moment while thinking of your Snapshots—your goals.
    *   ASK yourself, "Is what I am planning to do going to support my journey toward my goals?" Keep your Snapshots in mind.

8. If "Yes" is your answer,
    - DECIDE to
    - PROCEED with your intended behaviors.

9. If "No" is your answer,
    - ASK yourself, "Is what I am planning more important than my goals?"
      If you answer "No," then create alternatives that follow your goals.
    - Call on friends, or ask someone for help, if necessary.

10. If your answer is "Yes—what I am planning right now is more important than my goals," then…
    - drink a glass of water and
    - occupy yourself with another thought or activity for at least one minute before you
    - DECIDE to PROCEED with the unhelpful behavior.
    - BE SURE TO CONCENTRATE ON YOUR SNAPSHOTS BEFORE YOU DECIDE TO ABANDON YOUR GOALS!

11. If you did something that was not helpful toward your goals, admit that *you* chose to do it, study what happened, and learn from it. Then, move forward in a way that respects your renewed commitment

to yourself, to your goals, and to the contract with yourself.

- You are the most important person and friend to yourself.

12. Remember, this moment is all that counts! It is *now*. Consciously use the moment so that you can feel perfect within yourself, for yourself.

- Do not delude yourself by saying you will do something "just once," "just today," or you will "start after the weekend."
- Make each and every decision count so that you always move forward.
- The most important responsibility that you have to yourself is to live in the *now*! No other time exists.

$\mathscr{E}$XERCISE

$\mathscr{T}$HE MEMORY LEAF

1. You are CAGED if you believe that outside forces control you.
   - You can feel free and in control through
     Commitment,
     Awareness,
     Goals, and
     Exercise.
   - These four factors *Unlock Your CAGE*.

2. In truth, your CAGE does not exist unless you give it life.
   - You direct what you believe to exist.
   - You control your picture—
     What you think,
     What you feel, and
     What you do!

- You put on the eyeglasses that give you the images that you choose to see!

3. Mental exercise and physical exercise are your own best natural and innate contrasts. When one is in focus, the other lives in its background—like a frame and a canvas. The more that you focus on or exercise one, the clearer and stronger the other becomes when you look at it. Stepping away from thinking, feeling, and doing and moving to pure physical exercise give more strength to the mental exercises when you return to them.
    - Total involvement with one precludes the other, freeing you to experience your distinct energies.
    - Throughout each day, both physical and mental exercise must exist in order for each to exist, to be felt fully, and to be as deep and focused as you desire.

4. Select one or two physical activities—talents, capabilities, physical likes, or just desires—or simply select something that you would like to learn or to try.
    - Design a program for yourself based on your selections.
    - Enroll yourself in the program—in a formal contract or course, or in an informal contract with yourself or with a friend.

- Follow your program's design and make it an integral part of your daily activities.
- Do not break a contract with yourself!

5. At least once every day, before or after physical activity, spend time thinking about what you feel and your activity.
    - Renew your commitment to yourself.
    - Search for new understanding of an existing behavior that you may wish to change.
    - Analyze what you did and why you did it.
    - Change what you do and the way that you do it if you think it best.
    - Underscore or reset your goals.
    - Keep exercising your mind and body so that you feel energy.

6. At least once a week, and whenever you desire or feel the need, reread The Lessons and your notebook.
    - Share your experiences with friends if you feel comfortable doing so.

22575611R00070

Made in the USA
Middletown, DE
04 August 2015